JOURNALS FOR EVERYONE

MW01295809

Journals For Everyone
ISBN 10– 1986412652
ISBN 13 - 978-1986412650